First Facts®

Ada Lovelace

A 4D BOOK

by Mary Boone

CAPSTONE PRESS
a capstone imprint

This is a Capstone 4D book!

Want fun videos that go with this book?

Just visit www.capstone4d.com

Use this password
lovelace.27728

First Facts are published by Capstone Press
1710 Roe Crest Drive, North Mankato, Minnesota 56003
www.mycapstone.com

Library of Congress Cataloging-in-Publication Data
Names: Boone, Mary, 1963– author.
Title: Ada Lovelace : a 4D book / by Mary Boone.
Description: North Mankato, Minnesota : an imprint of Capstone Press, [2019] |
Series: First facts. STEM scientists and inventors | Audience: Ages 6-9. | Includes index.
Identifiers: LCCN 2018001965 (print) | LCCN 2018008545 (ebook) | ISBN 9781543527803 (eBook PDF) | ISBN 9781543527841 (ePub Fixed Layout) | ISBN 9781543527728 (hardcover) | ISBN 9781543527766 (pbk.)

Subjects: LCSH: Lovelace, Ada King, Countess of, 1815–1852—Juvenile literature. | Women mathematicians—Great Britain—Biography—Juvenile literature. | Women computer programmers—Great Britain—Biography—Juvenile literature. | Mathematicians—Great Britain—Biography—Juvenile literature. | Computer programmers—Great Britain—Biography—Juvenile literature. | Computers—Great Britain—History—19th century—Juvenile literature. Classification: LCC QA29.L72 (ebook) | LCC QA29.L72 B66 2018 (print) | DDC 510.92 [B]—dc23
LC record available at https://lccn.loc.gov/2018001965

Editorial Credits
Erika L. Shores and Jessica Server, editors; Charmaine Whitman, designer; Eric Gohl, media researcher; Laura Manthe, production specialist

Image Credits
Alamy: Colin Underhill, 19; Getty Images: Science & Society Picture Library, 15; Library of Congress: 7; New York Public Library: 6; Newscom: akg-images, 9, Heritage Images/The Print Collector, 13, UPPA/Photoshot, cover; Shutterstock: Golden Shrimp, cover & interior (backgrounds); Wikimedia: Public Domain, 5, 11, 17, 21

Printed in China.
XXXXXX

Table of Contents

CHAPTER 1

Birth of a Genius

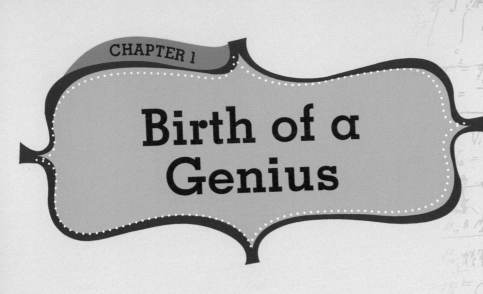

Ada Lovelace was born more than 200 years ago. But she played a big role in the way computers are used today. Others of her time were trying to build simple machines that could add numbers. But Ada knew with the right **programming**, these machines could do more than just math.

programming—writing instructions to make a machine or computer work in a certain way

Ada Lovelace

Augusta "Ada" Byron was born in London on December 10, 1815. Her father was the famous poet Lord Byron. He left his family when Ada was a baby. She never got to know her father. He died when she was 8 years old.

Ada as a child

graduate—to finish all the required classes at school

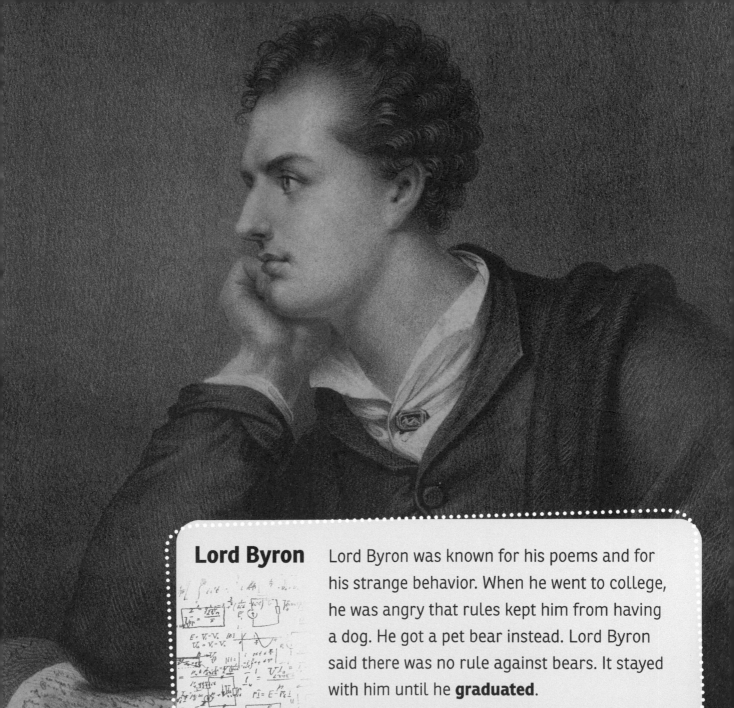

Lord Byron

Lord Byron was known for his poems and for his strange behavior. When he went to college, he was angry that rules kept him from having a dog. He got a pet bear instead. Lord Byron said there was no rule against bears. It stayed with him until he **graduated**.

Ada's mother, Anne Isabella Milbanke, was known as Lady Byron. Anne wanted her only child to get a good education. At the time, it was unusual for girls to study math and science. But that's exactly what Ada did.

FACT As a child, Ada was often sick. When she got the measles, she had to stay in bed for a year.

Anne Isabella Milbanke

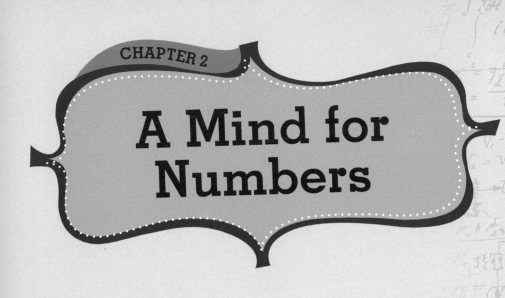

CHAPTER 2

A Mind for Numbers

Even as a child, it was easy to see Ada had a talent for both numbers and languages. By age 12, she had drawn detailed plans for a flying machine. Her design had a pair of giant wings. It was powered by a **steam engine**.

steam engine—an engine that gets power by heating water to make steam

"Religion to me is science, and science is religion."

Ada Lovelace

Ada's mother hired **tutors** to teach her. One tutor was **astronomer** and **mathematician** Mary Somerville. Somerville introduced 17-year-old Ada to mathematician and inventor Charles Babbage. Ada was very interested in Babbage's plan to build the "Difference Engine." He said it would be able to do difficult math problems.

tutor—a teacher who gives lessons to just one student or a small group of students

astronomer—a scientist who studies stars, planets, and other objects in space

mathematician—a person who studies math

Charles Babbage

Ada visited Babbage's home to watch him use his invention. The machine was made of a stack of numbered wheels. It was powered by the turn of a handle. Ada had questions and ideas about the invention. She began to write letters to Babbage. He soon became her **mentor**.

Speaking Out

Girls in the early 1800s were taught to keep their ideas to themselves. Ada Lovelace was smart and she knew it. She could not sit silently while men shared their ideas. Many people said Ada was rude because she spoke her mind.

mentor—a trusted teacher or guide

Babbage's Difference Engine

CHAPTER 3

The Lovelace Legacy

In 1834 Babbage invented a more advanced math machine. An article about the machine was written in French. Ada was asked to rewrite it in English. As she wrote, Ada added her own **formulas** for solving more difficult problems. She also made notes in the article. She wrote about ways in which formulas could be used as instructions to run the machine.

formula—a rule in science or math that is written with numbers and symbols

Diagram for the computation by the Engine of the Numbers of Bernoulli. See Note G. (page 722 *et seq.*)

[A large tabular diagram follows, with column groupings: "Data.", "Working Variables.", and "Result Variables."]

Number of Operation.	Nature of Operation.	Variables acted upon.	Variables receiving results.	Indication of change in the value on any Variable.	Statement of Results.	Data.			Working Variables.									Result Variables.			
						$^1V_1$	$^1V_2$	$^1V_3$	$^0V_4$	$^0V_5$	$^0V_6$	$^0V_7$	$^0V_8$	$^0V_9$	$^0V_{10}$	$^0V_{11}$	$^0V_{12}$	$^0V_{13}$	$^1V_{21}$ $^1V_{22}$ $^1V_{23}$ $^0V_{24}$
						1	2	n											B_1 B_3 B_5 B_7

a diagram from the article on Babbage's machine

FACT In Ada's notes, she also wrote about how machines might someday understand science and even create music.

Sadly, on November 27, 1852, Ada died from cancer at age 36. Nearly 100 years after her death, people who studied her work discovered how brilliant it was. People began to call her "the world's first computer programmer."

FACT Ada Lovelace Day is held every year on the second Tuesday of October. It celebrates women working in science, technology, engineering, and math.

Ada Augusta
Lovelace memorial
in Leicestershire,
England

Ada was a **pioneer** in computer programming. Her important work has been noted in books and movies. In 1980 the U.S. Department of Defense named its new computer language "Ada" after her. Ada Lovelace used math to make a difference in the world.

Family Life

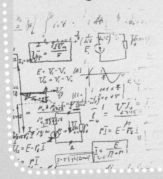

In 1835 Ada married William King. William was given a royal title in 1838. The couple became known as the "Earl and Countess of Lovelace." Ada and William's three children were Anne, Ralph, and Byron.

pioneer—a person who is the first to try new things

Ada in 1852

Glossary

astronomer (uh-STRAH-nuh-muhr)—a scientist who studies stars, planets, and other objects in space

formula (FOR-myuh-luh)—a rule in science or math that is written with numbers and symbols

graduate (GRAJ-oo-ayt)—to finish all the required classes at school

mathematician (MATH-uh-muh-tish-uhn)—a person who studies math

mentor (MEN-tur)—a trusted teacher or guide

pioneer (pye-uh-NEER)—a person who is the first to try new things

programming (PROH-gram-ing)—writing instructions to make a machine or computer work in a certain way

steam engine (STEEM EN-juhn)—an engine that gets power by heating water to make steam

tutor (TOO-tur)—a teacher who gives lessons to just one student or a small group of students

Read More

Stanley, Diane. *Ada Lovelace, Poet of Science: The First Computer Programmer*. New York: Simon & Schuster/Paula Wiseman Books, 2016.

Wallmark, Laurie. *Ada Byron Lovelace and the Thinking Machine*. Berkeley, Calif.: Creston Books, 2015.

Internet Sites

Use Facthound to find Internet sites related to this book.

Visit *www.facthound.com*

Just type in 9781543527728 and go!

 **Super-cool stuff!** Check out projects, games and lots more at **www.capstonekids.com**

Critical Thinking Questions

1. When Ada Lovelace was a child, most girls received little education. How different would the world be if girls today could not go to school?

2. Imagine you met Ada Lovelace at a party in 1843, and she told you about her ideas for a machine that could think. How would you have reacted?

Index